£3.99

HE LOST HIS TRANSFORMERS ANNUAL...

DON'T LOSE YOURS!

Make sure you hang on to your Annual by completing the space, right, with your name and address. That way everyone will know it's yours . . . and even rifts in time and space won't dare take it away from you!

THIS ANNUAL BELONGS TO . . .

NAME ....

ADDRESS ....

....

....

THE TRANSFORMERS™ ANNUAL, published 1989 by **MARVEL COMICS LTD.,** 13/15 Arundel Street, London WC2R 3DX. **THE TRANSFORMERS** (including all prominent characters featured in this Annual), and the distinctive likenesses thereof are trademarks of **Hasbro Inc.** All TRANSFORMERS material is copyright © 1989 Hasbro Inc. All rights reserved. All other material is copyright © 1989 Marvel Comics Ltd. All rights reserved. No similarity between any of the names, characters, persons and/or institutions in this Annual with any living or dead person and/or institution is intended, and any such similarity which may exist is purely coincidental Printed in Italy.

TRANSFORMERS ANNUAL

·CONTENTS·

If you've picked up this Annual feeling somewhat on the cynical side, don't worry. Even we – the creative team – wondered exactly how we could top last year's veritable feast of Transformers action and excitement. Well, we weren't about to let the enormity of our task get the better of us, and the Annual you now hold is a testament to what we – modestly – consider to be success beyond our wildest imaginings! This year's *Transformers Annual* is not only better than last year's, it's much better! First off we've three slices of strip that are so hot, you'd best be careful not to burn yourself as you turn the pages. The trio – *Destiny Of The Dinobots, Dreadwing Down,* and *The Chain Gang* – have more thrills and shocks per frame than ever before! Add to this a text thriller that charts the course of the Transformers war as never before, and a two part text shocker entitled *Trigger-Happy* and you've got an Annual to savour again and again! Oh, did we forget to mention pages of fact-files (featuring the incredible Micromasters), puzzles and posters? Yep, thought we did! Enjoy the Annual, folks, and don't forget the action continues every week in Marvel's *Transformers* weekly comic!

·CONTENTS·CONTENTS·

Editor: **Chris Francis** · Designer: **Gary Gilbert** · Cover Art: **Lee Sullivan**
Inside cover art: **Wetherell/ Baskerville/ Burns**

THE QUEST! ▶ ▶ ▶ ▶ ▶ ▶

The holo-head of the teacher was speaking, and though his mind was elsewhere, Dicet managed to take in what it was saying.

" . . . and so, pupils, your assigned task for the tri-annual rest period, is to present a detailed dissertation on a major inter-planetary war, from within the last six gluxins . . ."

'Rest period' scoffed Dicet, returning – with great effort – his full attention to the learning dais and the image thereon. 'Maybe it's a rest period for the teachers, but for us it's four anns of unmitigated hard slog!' Angrily, Dicet drove a fist through the light image, interrupting its monotonous recitation not a jot.

" . . . projects will be prepared in solid light form and encapsulated on the brainwave encoder by . . ."

Realising that the holo-image would have its say whether he liked it or not, Dicet decided to remove himself from the im-mediate vicinity. He knew how long he had to complete his project – *not long enough!* As he rolled off his scoop and descended the anti-grav pads to the crystalline floor of his family's culture pod, Dicet tried again to stir up some enthusiasm for ancient inter-planetary war. In a world where his only brush with combat thus far had been with his mother concerning his regular steam clean (she'd won!), wars on distant planets in even more distant pasts, where beings were injured and even died, seemed remote and unreal. What was it the holo-teacher had told him, after absorbing and discard-ing his last travesty (the teacher's words) of an ancient war project? Ah yes – 'pupil Dicet needs to get more actively involved in this subject'.

Ever one to take people at their word, Dicet decided the only possible way he was going to stir up enthusiasm for this latest project, was to do just that – involve himself active-ly! As he stared out across the undulating white vistas of Theturis's plasma plains, he racked his brain for a war that even remote-ly interested him. Ah, yes – he had it. A small, but bitterly fought war had once raged between two factions of mechanical beings. Though originally a civil war – confined to . . . 'ah, what was the name of the place? Er, Cycatron? Cybertron, that's it.' Though originally confined to the metal world of Cybertron, the . . . er, Transfor-mers' war spread to a small carbon-based planet named Earth. Robots with the ability to transform into likenesses of Earth's vehi-cles, machinery and weapons. Now that, Dicet decided, was interesting. Of course, interesting as it was, the subject's appeal would wane geometrically each hour he spent in the knowledge module, staring at endless history tapes. No, if he was going to learn anything about the Transformers' war, he was going to have to actually be there, watching it happen!

Prepared with a date by date progression of the Autobot/Decepticon (as the two fac-tions were named) War and an event recor-der, Dicet stepped warily into the Trans-time Pod. Programmed into its circuits were nine key moments – culled from the date by date – in the conflict. The pod would transport him through time and space to those exact moments, so he could witness first hand the turning points in the Transformers' war. Dicet nervously slid the seal door closed. The Transtime Pod was strictly out of bounds to him. As his father was keen on saying, 'it's not a toy!' Indeed, according to his father the device was not even properly tested yet. It had been en-trusted to Dicet's father – a key theoreti-cian in advanced sci-mechanics – for final checks. Well, thought Dicet, swallowing a nervous gulp, it's certainly going to get tested now. Before he could have second thoughts (well, fourth thoughts by this time!), Dicet triggered the device. There was a low hum that seemed to build in intensity from within him, rather than from within the machine, a strong smell reminis-cent of bad eggs, and – in a blinding flash of light – he was gone into the past . . .

A HISTORY OF THE AUTOBOT/ DECEPTICON WAR By Dicet Alpha-zero

Suddenly it's 1st Cycle 931 (Cybertronian dating) and I'm aboard the Autobots' vast star-ship, The Ark, careening out of control through space. A simple cloaking screen keeps me from being seen, but to be honest I imagine that both factions have more press-ing matters on their minds. The battle is awesome! The Autobots (weary after their efforts to save Cybertron) stand their ground against the Decepticons who have breached the Ark's outer hull. Though several Auto-bots seem to acknowledge that they are badly outnumbered and outgunned, they fight on – seemingly more determined than

field. The Ark was built, and Optimus Prime led a group of the greatest Autobot warriors into space. For days they laboured to blast a path through the asteroid field, and finally they succeeded – safeguarding their world. But Megatron too had built a craft, and led the Decepticons into space. Ever the opportunist, he had guessed correctly that the Autobots would be exhausted and unprepared for battle.

I guess we must be in the vicinity of Earth by now, because Prime and Prowl, two of the last Autobots left standing, have backed away into the control room, pinned down by the Decepticon firepower. It's at this point that Prime tells Prowl he cannot allow Megatron his victory. Plotting a collision course with Earth, Prime blows the Ark's main engines. There's a savage rush of G forces as the Ark drops through space. I see Megatron as he enters the chamber, realising in a moment of shocked horror that Prime has sacrificed the Autobots to end his menace forever! I see Prime's triumphant look, and then activate the 'jump' circuits, leaving before the Ark can imbed itself beneath a dormant volcano on Earth, where it will remain for the next four million years – a tomb for the Autobots and the Decepticons.

ever. And there's the reason. At the heart of the fighting, swatting Decepticons aside like Funari flies, is their leader – Optimus Prime! His dedication to the heroic Autobots' cause rallies his troops' flagging spirits – driving them to the limits of endurance and beyond. Before, I couldn't have imagined a being who could inspire such respect, but actually seeing him . . . well, you'll just have to take my word on this . . . you realise he's all the history tapes say he was and more! Trouble is, the Transformer leading the Decepticons is more than a match for him in terms of power and sheer evil might. With one blow, Megatron pulps two Autobots, shredding a third with a blast from his fusion cannon. Each time he fires that thing, it's like a Hydrus bomb going off in a cramped life pod! I skirt around the periphery of the battle (carefully!), making my way towards the main control chamber, where I know Prime will soon make the fateful decision that will involve Earth in the Autobot/Decepticon war.

As I enter the chamber – ahead of Prowl and Prime – I review the events that led to this outer space battle. Some years into the civil war on Cybertron, Autobot scientists discovered that their world (shaken loose from its orbit by the sheer scale of the combat) was on a collision course with a vast asteroid

THE QUEST! ▶ ▶ ▶ ▶ ▶ ▶

I'm on Earth (1984 by their reckoning) before my last thought's completed. I've arrived in the Ark in the midst of an argument between the Autobots, Huffer and Ironside. Since I was last around, the Ark's long dormat computers have been reactivated, both factions of Transformers have been re-built with the ability to transform into likenesses of Earth's vehicles, machinery and weaponry, and the battle has begun anew on Earth. The subject of the argument is Sparkplug Witwicky, father of Buster (who saved the Autobot, Bumblebee's life). Sparkplug had offered to supply a fuel conversion formula that would render Earth's fuel usable by the Autobots. Kidnapped by Megatron and taken to the Decepticons' fortress base, Sparkplug was forced to reveal the formula to the Decepticons. Huffer evidently isn't too wowed about that, and Ironside's defending Sparkplug. While they're arguing, I notice Sparkplug and Buster start to sneak away, wisely deciding to let the Autobots sort it out between themselves. Before they can get clear, Jazz's flame-thrower blocks their way. Startled, Sparkplug suffers a mild heart attack. Transforming to ambulance mode, Ratchet whizzes him towards the hospital. I'm tempted to tell Buster his Dad'll be fine, but I know better than to interfere.

I hang around, watching as Huffer tells Prime of the existence of five Autobots, collectively known as the Dinobots, and a probe is despatched to Antarctica to find them. I'm not really interested. I'll be meeting the Dinobots in person later – so this is really no big deal. Finally, it happens – ennervated by Sparkplug's fuel, Megatron and the Decepticons attack. As before, it's the Autobots who fall. Just as Megatron's thinking he's finally won, they all keel over and collapse helpless to the ground. It's fun to watch, I can tell you! You see, what Megatron didn't realise was that Sparkplug had poisoned the fuel he made for the Decepticons; adding a corrosive element to it. Pretty sneaky, huh? After a while, the fuel ate through their fuel lines and into their circuitry. The Autobots get to their feet, and my shout of warning dies in my throat. I watch helplessly as the wall explodes inwards, felling the Autobots. Just before I blink out again, I see the Decepticon, Shockwave, standing over the Autobots, his single eye glowing brightly!

As I appear at the edge of a marsh, a few months later, I chide myself for even thinking about trying to warn Prime. What's past is past. I hate to think what would happen if I inadvertently changed the course

of history. So what's been happening? Well, Shockwave took control of the Decepticons, using the head of Optimus Prime (and the Autobots' sacred life-force, the Creation Matrix, therein) to create new Decepticons, and Ratchet – after finding and restoring the Dinobots – defeated Megatron and managed to free and reactivate all the Autobots. I watch as Sideswipe and Prowl are gunned down by their own leader, Optimus Prime! They and other Autobots had come here expecting to find the missing head of their leader, and instead found a Prime head left as trap by Shockwave. The head's a fake, and it guides Prime's body for the Decepticons. But help is at hand in the shape of Buster Witwicky. Using the Creation Matrix that Prime stowed in his mind, Buster takes control of the recently created Decepticon, Jetfire, and gets him to take Prime's real head to his body. After that it's all over bar the shouting. Reunited with his body at last, Prime soon sorts out Shockwave. Safe in the knowledge that Jetfire will become an Autobot and Prime's gonna' reclaim the Autobot leadership and the Creation Matrix, I blink out again.

A quick stop here. It's really just to witness first hand the arrival of the future Decepticon, Galvatron, on present day Earth. An awful lot of the upcoming problems for the Autobots (and for the Decepticons, for that matter!) are gonna' be caused by this guy, so it's worth seeing him turn up. The way it works is this. In the year 2006, a badly injured Megatron is re-made as Galvatron by a planet-sized Transformer called Unicron. Things didn't go too well for Galvatron, so he decides he's better off in 1986 (a time he visited before when he plotted to destroy Unicron). I hang around long enough to watch Galvatron trash a human built mechanoid called Centurion (an action that will bring him into conflict with the Dinobots) and then I'm on my way again.

It's only a short hop this time. Just far enough forwards in time to see the climactic confrontration between Optimus Prime and Megatron. This isn't going to be pleasant (seeing as I already know what's going to happen), but I have to see this first hand – experience it! We're in the building that houses computer programmer Ethan Zachary's software business. Zachary had stumbled into a battle between Prime (backed up by the Protectobots) and Megatron (with the Combaticons in tow). With the battle deadlocked, both leaders accepted Ethan's novel solution. Prime and Megatron would battle to the death within the

framework of his computer game, Multi-world. They stand there, hooked into the system by way of wires leading to their neural circuits. On the screen, the computer's version of Prime has just been tricked by its version of Megatron (in other words, Megatron cheated). But, against all the odds, Prime wins – sending Megatron plunging to his computerised doom. All well and good, except that in doing so, Prime inadvertently killed some of Multi-World's inhabitants. As Prime and Megatron return to their bodies, Prime refuses to accept his victory. Prime went against all he stands for – sacrificing innocent beings in order to win a battle. I watch Ethan's despair as Prime tells him to terminate his life functions. He hesitates, but Prime is adamant. Zachary throws the switch and Optimus Prime explodes – blown into hundreds of pieces. I have to fight back the tears as one of the noblest beings I've ever encountered dies. Of course, I'm heartened by the knowledge that Zachary has Prime's personality on computer floppy disc. As Megatron triumphantly turns away, I look forward to seeing Prime's re-birth on Nebulos in a couple of jumps time.

In the meantime, though, I look in on Mount Verona, some months later. For a moment I think I've arrived too late, but then I see it. Perched atop the Mount Verona is a vast ring of machinery – built by Galvatron to harness the energy of the Earth's core. At this point in time, Galvatron's several circuits short of a diode, and has devised this insane scheme to transform himself into a god! Things look pretty bleak. The future Autobots, Rodimus Prime, Kup and Blurr, along with their ally, Wreck-Gar, and the robotic bounty-hunter, Death's Head, have been whisked off to their own time, mistakenly thinking that Galvatron would be returned with them. Not so. And with Ultra Magnus seemingly buried under molten lava, only the Throttlebot, Goldbug, stands between Galvatron and total victory. Knowing better, I move to the edge of the volcano to watch the final phase of this battle. Clawing his way up the inside of the volcano (from the narrow ledge he landed on after being thrown in by Galvatron) is the Cybertronian Autobots' greatest warrior, Ultra Magnus. Before I realise what's happening, I'm swaying dizzily. The intense heat from the volcano has left me weak and unsteady on my feet. With horror, I realise I'm pitching forwards into the volcano. I hit metal and I realise with almost greater horror I've landed on the emerging Ultra Magnus's head. His tired eyes roll upwards, surprised. I panic, I trigger the 'jump' ahead of schedule and disappear.

I'm on the planet Nebulos before I realise I've even triggered the device. I sit down, my reeling mind trying to take in the closeness of death, and the enormity of what I almost let happen. If I'd died then – years out of my own time and on a strange world – I'd have altered the shape of space and time as surely as the future Decepticon, Cyclonus, will soon do. And what of Ultra Magnus? Did he notice me? Did his surprise cause him to let go and plunge to his death in the volcano? Ultra Magnus has to survive in order to defeat Galvatron. He later sacrifices himself to destroy Galvatron's machine and bury them both under molten lava. Have I altered the course of history? I try not to think of the consequences if I have. I may return to my own time and planet to find that I no longer exist, or my world irrevocably and terribly changed. The only sure way seems to be to press on and see for myself. The time-jump after next will reveal what's happening on Earth. I'm not looking forward to finding out. In the meantime, I decide I might as well see what I came to see. This is Nebulos, another planet which the warring Transformers spread their conflict to. As a gesture of peace, the Autobot commander, Fortress Maximus, ordered his newly arrived forces to surrender to the Nebulans and remove their heads. When Scorponok and his Decepticons arrived in pursuit, they found Nebulos to be virtually undefended. Until, that is, the Nebulan scientists found a way to bio-engineer their bodies to transform into likenesses of the Autobots' heads. They became Headmasters – Nebulan and Autobot in control of one united Transformer body. Targetmasters (where the Nebulan transforms to become the Transformer's gun) followed, and soon a whole new war had begun. Autobot and Decepticon Headmasters and Targetmasters slugging it out, and wrecking a goodly portion of the planet in the process. In order to save their planet, the Autobots fled – heading for Earth – and the Decepticons followed. But that's old hat – I'm here to see the construction of a new breed of Nebulan Transformers – Powermasters. Goldbug, Slapdash, Getaway and Joyride came here hoping to find a way to restore Optimus Prime to life, using Nebulan skills and technology. They succeeded. I watch as Optimus Prime – Powermaster – swings into battle against the Decepticon Powermasters, Dreadwind and Darkwing. Even if I didn't know the outcome, I'd have confidently put my money on Prime to win. With the Nebulan, HiQ, transforming to become Prime's engine, and supplying him with power, it's a foregone conclusion.

I beat Prime back to Earth (several months later) to see him confront Dinobot commander, Grimlock, who's taken the Autobot leadership in Prime's absence. Neither he, nor the other Dinobots – Slag, Sludge, Swoop and Snarl – are very happy about this, but Prime sweet-talks them. Before they realise what's happening, they're following Prime's orders. I smile, relaxing. Things don't *seem* to have altered.

My final visit takes me right into the heart of the end of the world! Because of Cyclonus' death, twenty years out of his time, the very fabric of time and space is falling apart. A gaping rift in time is tearing Earth apart. I look around at the carnage. Autobot and Decepticon bodies lie around, dead and dying. I count at least twelve down or on the critical list just in the immediate vicinity. I see Ultra Magnus (of the year 2009) lying on the ground, practically gutted. Rodimus Prime's got his hands full battling a fighting mad Megatron, but Optimus Prime's got the toughest job of all. I look at the snarling, insane Galvatron and wonder how he can still be functioning. Half his face is gone, and a lot of the back of his head is missing. He's dented, blasted and trailing wires and circuitry. And yet still he fights on – like a mad dog, too far gone to realise it's dying. Against such raw, naked savagery, Optimus Prime is hard pressed to stay alive. Then suddenly there's an inhuman howl of fury from Galvatron. I look up to see what he's seen and pale in shock. The sky has opened a seething mouth of unearthly ener-

gy, and suddenly we're all being drawn towards it. The rift in time and space has become a tangible, physical thing – and it's hungry! Like King Canute of old Earth legends, Galvatron stands in front of it, howling defiance. I watch nauseated as the vortex strips Galvatron to the exo-skeleton, and then swallows what's left with hardly a pause. Still the maelstrom continues, and I wonder if I'm going to end up in there as well. As Prime throws what's left of Scourge into the maw of the distortion, there's a physical sensation of abatement, but no real let-up. Like some demanding god, the rift demands more sacrifice. Saviours come in unlikely shapes and forms, but the ex-Decepticon leader, Shockwave, is surely the unlikeliest saviour of all. Nevertheless, just when everyone's figured they're on the way out, Shockwave jets in in space gun mode, depositing the remains of Cyclonus into the heart of the rift. It's like someone's turned off a switch. Suddenly there's just this really oppressive silence. It's over, but no-one's kidding themselves it'll ever be the same again! I skip the aftermath and blink out, for the last time.

Dicet Alpha-zero. 123/9/005

Dicet stared glumly at the recently incinerated remains of his essay, wondering what to do. He'd watched horror-struck as his father had fed the carefully prepared report of the Transformers war into the microwave disposal unit. He'd never seen his father so cold, so obsessively furious. When he'd discovered that Dicet had used the Transtime Pod, his father had done an excellent impression of a rift in time and space, practically shredding him to his exo-skeleton. Okay, he'd disobeyed his father's strict orders and tampered with the Transtime Pod. Okay, his father was annoyed because the government had decided to scrap the project – considering it too dangerous after reading Dicet's own school project. Okay, so his father had lost valuable credits and face over the matter. But still, his reaction had seemed like that of a different man altogether. As Dicet wondered what he was going to tell his holo-teachers the next day (not the truth – that was sure!), a far more unpleasant thought began to rear its ugly head. What if he *had* altered history . . . even in a tiny, almost unnoticeable way? Was this the father he'd left a few days before? Was this the world he'd left a few days before? Dicet shivered, suddenly feeling very alone in a world he'd once felt so comfortable in . . .

THE END!

EARTH, 1992 — ANTARCTICA.

THEY CALL THIS PLACE THE SAVAGE LAND...

DINOBOTS — WE'RE UNDER ATTACK!

ASSUME DEFENSIVE FORMATION! KEEP THEM AWAY FROM *SNARL*!

KRAK!

SURE, *GRIMLOCK*! AND WHILE WE'RE DOING THAT, THESE PREHISTORIC PEA-BRAINS'LL TRAMPLE US TO *IRON FILINGS*!

SPEAK FOR YOURSELF, *SLAG*. UNTIL MY ADVER-SARIES INVENT AIR TRAFFIC CONTROL...

DESTINY of the DINOBOTS!

Dinosaur consultant/Plot/Colour **STEVE WHITE**

Plot/Script **STEVE ALAN**

Art **ANDY WILDMAN**

Letters **GLIB**

THE DINOBOTS ARE ABOUT TO DISCOVER WHY!

THEY'RE JUST FLYING BLIND!

TH A W!

GO EASY ON THEM, SWOOP. I DON'T THINK IT'S AN ATTACK AS SUCH! WE JUST GOT IN THE WAY OF A STAMPEDE!

UH UH, FELLA...

THAT'S AS CLOSE AS YOU GET...

WOK!

...TO MY POOR, *SICK* BUDDY, *SNARL!*

CORRODIA GRAVIS - MOLECULAR BREAKDOWN OF HIS COMPONENT METALS. WHAT A *LOUSY* WAY TO GO!

GOT THAT RIGHT, *SLUDGE*. SO LET'S GET ON WITH FINDING THE ONE THING THAT COULD SAVE HIM - THE *CONTROL CRYSTAL!*

THIS WAY WE CAN AT LEAST SAVE HIS *MIND* WHILE WE FIND HIM A NEW BODY. THE CRYSTAL WILL STORE HIS BRAINWAVES AND -

WHOA THERE! WE DON'T EVEN KNOW WHERE THE CRYSTAL IS!

" WHEN WE LOCATED THE SHUTTLE THAT BROUGHT US HERE ALL THOSE YEARS AGO *, THE CENTRAL CONTROL CRYSTAL - PERHAPS THE LAST IN EXISTENCE ..."

* *TRANSFORMERS 7.*

"...HAD GONE!"

THANKFULLY, WHILE IT'S STILL ACTIVE, OUR INTERNAL CIRCUITS CAN TRACK IT -

HEY- *WHAT'S THIS?*

16

ANYONE HOME?

THUNCH

AWW NO! A HUMAN! I'VE HAD IT UP TO HERE WITH YOU BOTHERSOME BIPEDS!

RUDIMENTRY SPEECH CIRCUITS. FASCINATING! ALLOW ME TO INTRODUCE MYSELF... EMBREY'S THE NAME, PROFESSOR EMBREY. I'M A PALEONTOLOGIST.

NOW, WHAT DO YOU MEAN BY ATTACKING MY DINOSAURS?

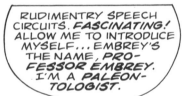

YOUR DINOSAURS? LOOK, I DON'T KNOW WHAT YOU'RE DOING HERE, OR WHY YOU SHOT AT US, BUT—

THE CONTROL CRYSTAL!

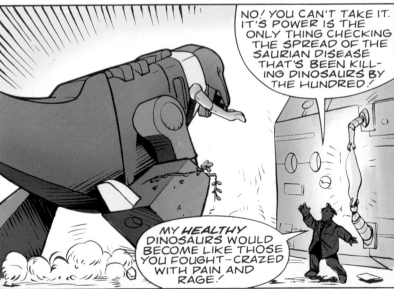

NO! YOU CAN'T TAKE IT. IT'S POWER IS THE ONLY THING CHECKING THE SPREAD OF THE SAURIAN DISEASE THAT'S BEEN KILLING DINOSAURS BY THE HUNDRED!

MY HEALTHY DINOSAURS WOULD BECOME LIKE THOSE YOU FOUGHT—CRAZED WITH PAIN AND RAGE!

18

LOOK, I'M SORRY I SHOT AT YOU, BUT I THOUGHT YOU MEANT US HARM. DON'T TAKE THE CRYSTAL, *PLEASE!*

WE CAN'T TAKE THE CRYSTAL, GRIMLOCK. NOT IF IT CONDEMNS INNOCENT CREATURES TO DEATH!

BUT WITHOUT IT, SNARL WILL *DIE!*

MAYBE NOT. I'VE AN IDEA SO SNEAKY YOU COULD PIN A PURPLE BADGE ON IT AND CALL IT DECEPTICON!

LATER... WHAT'S A PALEONTOLOGIST SLAG?

SOMEONE WHO STUDIES DINOSAURS, SLUDGE. *SHH.*

IT'S DONE.

YOU MEAN... SNARL'S MIND IS IN *THAT?*

YEP. THE CONTROL CRYSTAL ABSORBED THE ESSENCE OF HIS MIND AND TRANSFERRED IT TO THE *STEGOSAURUS!*

AT LEAST WE'VE SAVED HIS LIFE!

LATER STILL...

HOW MUCH DO YOU RECKON HE'LL REMEMBER?

NOT MUCH, MAYBE *ENOUGH.* EMBREY'LL KEEP HIM SAFE UNTIL WE FIND A NEW BODY FOR HIM. BUT WHATEVER HE REMEMBERS, WHATEVER HE LOOKS LIKE...

...WE'LL ALWAYS BE A DINOBOT!

THE END!

19

THE AUTOBOT VERSUS DECEPTICON

This year's Annual has a Transformers quiz with a difference! It's time to find out exactly where your sympathies lie. Are you an Autobot supporter or a Decepticon supporter? Do you side with the forces of good, led by the noblest Autobot of all, Optimus Prime, or do you have a secret urge to join Scorponok's Decepticons? Here's your chance to take an active part in the Autobot/Decepticon war, as we stage a battle of wits between the two forces! The amount of Transformers knowledge you possess, the better your chosen side will fare! You can find out how to join in by reading the rules of battle on the facing page …

AUTOBOT A:
Q.1) Whose hand pressed the button that sent the Ark hurtling towards Earth four million years ago?
Q.2) Name the Autobot surgeon responsible for handing Megatron one of his greatest defeats and freeing the captive Autobots.
Q.3) What was Shockwave seeking when he captured Optimus Prime and separated his head from his body?

AUTOBOT B:
Q.1) What was the name of Ark's sentient computer that re-built the wrecked Transformers?
Q.2) Which Dinobot transforms into a likeness of the long extinct dinosaur known as a Pteranadon?
Q.3) The leader of the Protectobots is Hotspot. but what type of vehicle does he transform into?

AUTOBOT C:
Q.1) The human built mechanoid know as Centurion once challenged the might of Megatron. But which Transformer destroyed him?
Q.2) Who destroyed Bumblebee and what name did Bumblebee assume when he was re-built?
Q.3) Which human was indirectly responsible for the death of Optimus Prime, after a battle in a computer game?

AUTOBOT D:
Q.1) What was the name of the planet-devouring Transformer who threatened future Cybertron?
Q.2) Which young Autobot became leader in 2006, and what name did he assume once transformed by the Creation Matrix?
Q.3) The death of which future Decepticon opened a rift in space and time?

–DUEL OF WITS!

Rules Of Battle: It helps, for obvious reasons, if two players (or two teams) take part in this duel of wits, but there's no reason why an individual can't take both sides, basically fighting him or herself. For the purposes of this explanation we shall assume there are two players. One player takes the side of the Autobots (questions on the left hand page), the other takes the side of the Decepticons (questions below). To begin the game, the Autobot must identify his first warrior (pic A on his side of the gameboard) correctly. He then asks his Decepticon opponent that warrior's three questions. The Decepticon scores for each he answers correctly. Then it's the Decepticon's turn to identify his first warrior and ask that warrior's three questions. As before, the Autobot scores for each he answers correctly. The Autobot then identifies his next warrior, and so on down the line, alternating between Autobot and Decepticon. The winner of the battle is the player with the most points. Failure to identify a warrior correctly gives victory to your opponent.

DECEPTICON A:
Q.1) What natural disaster once threatened Cybertron from space, and caused the Autobots to build the Ark?
Q.2) Name the Decepticons' master of stealth and spy supreme.
Q.3) What type of gun did the Ark's computer give Megatron the ability to transform into?

DECEPTICON B:
Q.1) Which two Decepticon tape cassettes transform into bird-like creatures (other than Ratbat)?
Q.2) Who supplied the corrosive fuel that caused the Decepticons to fall in defeat?
Q.3) Brawl, Onslaught, Swindle, and Blast Off. Name the missing Combaticon and the giant robot the five combine to form.

DECEPTICON C:
Q.1) Two future Decepticons travelled back in time to become Targetmasters. Name their Nebulan companions.
Q.2) What is the combined jet form of the two Decepticon Powermasters, Dreadwind and Darkwing?
Q.3) How did the Decepticon leader known as lord Straxus attempt to escape his all but destroyed body?

DECEPTICON D:
Q.1) Who took over as Decepticon leader of 2008 after Shockwave was terminated?
Q.2) What race tried to capture Earth and Cybertron of 2008 after their planet was destroyed?
Q.3) Name Earth's unlikely saviour who sealed the growing rift in time and space.

"Those lights! Gotta get out of those lights!" yelled Backstreet. His tyres screeched on the tarmac as he accelerated and began to zig-zag. Despite his desperate efforts, however, his sports car chassis stayed fixed in the glare of his pursuers' headlights.

The panicked Autobot applied still more power, aware that he was already moving too fast along the winding, mountain road. "Who's on to me?" he asked himself fearfully. "Is it humans, the Decepticons, or – even worse – is it the Autobots?"

The split-second he spent considering his own question was a fatal lapse of concentration. He was suddenly on a tight bend, and still gaining speed! Pure instinct told the Triggerbot to slam on his brakes, but his actions merely threw him into a spin. His tyres shrieked and lost all grip as he corkscrewed around. The edge of the mountain road – and the black unknown beyond – hurtled towards him. Howling in fear, the Autobot vehicle left the road and began plummeting into the darkness.

"Hey – where'd he go?" asked Getaway as he and Joyride sped around the mountain bend.

"Must have, y'know, took off into the night. Used some of that scintillating acceleration of his," Joyride answered.

Getaway snorted in annoyance. "Terrific! Prime's going to be furious if we've let him give us the slip."

"I know our leader wants Backstreet brought in real bad," Joyride sighed, "but we weren't sure that it was our renegade friend anyway." The two Autobot Powermasters continued up the mountain and into the night. Neither saw the skid marks which had been Backstreet's last contact with the road before he'd spiralled from it.

His fingers felt as though they were on fire. Any second now they'd go into spasm; he'd lose his grip and fall into oblivion. "Hang on! Hang on just one more minute!" Backstreet pleaded with himself. He needed to be sure Getaway and Joyride were well away before he attempted scrambling back to the road five metres above. Otherwise his last ditch efforts in transforming to robot mode as he flew from the road, reaching to catch a mountainside tree stump, would be wasted.

"Enough!" he finally yelled. He fired the proton cannons on each of his shoulders. The kick-back gave him just enough impetus to lever against the tree stump, and haul himself upwards. Clawing finger holds and kicking foot holds, he battled frantically against gravity and the sheer mountainside.

Only when he found he was making horizontal not vertical progress did he realise he'd won, and was safely back on the roadside. He drew deep mechanical lungfuls of air. Another small victory in his campaign for survival. What kind of existence was it, though, he wondered, if staying alive long enough to draw his next breath was the summit of his ambition? How had he, a once proud member of Optimus Prime's Autobots, come to view his former friends with such fear and dread?

The ambush. Of course, the ambush! He hadn't forgotten, merely pushed it out of his mind. The botched attempt to capture the Decepticons, Crankcase and Ruckus. The Autobots had intercepted a message from them to their leader, Megatron. They had details of attack plans formulated by Scorponok's faction of Decepticons. The Autobots, the obvious targets for a Scorponok offensive, wanted to know those attack plans too. Prime had acted quickly, utilising the Earthly disguises of Landfill, Quickmix and Scoop to spring a trap. Looking like road construction vehicles, the three Double Targetmasters were in position to block the route taken by Crankcase and Ruckus. Prime, Dogfight and Override were hiding just off the road, ready to snare the Decepticons when they slowed down. And he, Backstreet, was the look out.

As radio silence was being maintained to prevent the Decepticons discovering the Autobot presence, Backstreet was to use a signalling device to alert Prime when the Decepticon pair came into view. This he'd done when he had observed them from his high vantage point above the settlement the humans called Rivers' Town.

Prime's orders to Backstreet were quite clear once he'd triggered the signal – he was to maintain surveillance in case more Decepticons were following. If any were observed, Backstreet was to use his devastating roadspeed to race down to the others and warn them. On no account was he to engage the enemy, as such actions could endanger the occupants of Rivers' Town.

Backstreet had followed his orders to the letter until he spotted Needlenose, Spinister and Windsweeper flying in low. The Decepticon aircraft looked very menacing, presenting Backstreet with a real dilemma. He believed he could outrun Spinister, the Double Targetmaster helicopter, but would the two jets reach him before he could warn Prime? And even though he was convinced he could take out both planes with surprise shots from his laser-guided proton missile cannons, he was under orders not to do so because of the town.

With mounting panic, Backstreet had watched the three airborne Decepticons

cruise towards Prime and the others. "A moment's indecision can be your last," he'd told himself many times, and without thought for the consequences, the Trigger-bot suddenly blasted away with his proton weapons. He'd fired well clear of the town – and the Decepticons – hoping his actions would alert Prime and the others to the impending danger. But Backstreet had merely succeeded in giving his position away to the Decepticons, who immediately pounded away at his cliff-top vantage point. Under such pressure, the Autobot found himself firing back blindly, his instincts of survival usurping any concern for the innocent humans and their town.

Whether Crankcase and Ruckus heard the firefight, or whether they were alerted by one of the Decepticon aircraft, Back-street never knew. But when he saw them hurtling away from the ambush zone, he guessed it had all gone wrong.

The bombardment from the Decepticon aircraft was at its height when Override had suddenly appeared. Backstreet remembered that Override's role called for him to assist Backstreet as early as possible, and the besieged Triggerbot was more than pleased to see his two-wheeled friend. However, Override brought nothing but bad news.

Backstreet was in big trouble. Backstreet had wrecked the ambush. Backstreet had infuriated Prime by disobeying direct orders. Worst of all, it seemed that blasts from his skirmish with the Decepticons had hit Rivers' Town! Backstreet had caused human casualties by his actions.

Despite Backstreet's attempts to explain that it had all been a horrible accident, Override hadn't let up hounding him for his mistakes, heightening the hapless Trigger-bot's panic. Both were still under fire from the Decepticons and Backstreet's nerves were stretched to breaking point. They had finally snapped when Override suggested he would probably face a court martial. He'd tried to act responsibly, tried to help others as best he could, but they were going to put him on trial for it. They'd find him guilty, make him the scapegoat by heaping all the blame on him for everything that had gone wrong. And then, they'd probably terminate him!

It had been too much for Backstreet to bear. With Decepticon laser cannon fire exploding all around, he'd seized the chance to make a break for it. A lightning transformation to car mode, an extended burst of his rear rocket thrusters, and Backstreet was away.

Now, after more than two days on the run, perched on an isolated mountain road, Backstreet was exhausted, lonely and very scared. On this strange, alien planet, the Autobot was friend to no-one, enemy to everyone. The humans wanted him for the damage to Rivers' Town. The Decepticons sought him as an eternal and natural foe. And the Autobots were hunting him, at the very least for desertion, and probably for much more!

Pin-pricks of light further down the mountain road caught Backstreet's attention. Headlights. Several vehicles, all coming his way – all coming for him! He swallowed hard and tasted fear as he steeled himself for another showdown. He began to wonder who it might be with, then realised it scarcely mattered.

"We have to find him soon, before anyone else does," mused Prime at the head of the Autobot search party. "In his panicked, confused state he's his own worst enemy. There's no telling what damage he may cause. . ."

"What'll happen once we catch him?" asked Override a little tentatively. "He disobeyed your direct orders after all."

"I know," Prime answered, "but despite that I won't pre-judge the issue until I've heard his side of the story. I also want to know why he ran like that. Am I such an ogre that he dare not face me when things go wrong. . ?"

"Gee, Boss – we was real scared you'd blow a dozen diodes when you heard we was nearly ambushed," chuckled Ruckus nervously.

On the seat of his battle-scarred buggy form was Megatron. He was in gun mode, and Ruckus' comment triggered a chilling, menacing laugh from the Walther P-38. "The Megatron of old might have reacted that way, but I am at last free of the madness that once clouded my mind. The incident was but an inconvenience. If we act quickly we can turn the entire episode to our considerable advantage."

"I don't get it, boss," put in Quake, the powerful Decepticon Double Targetmaster, rumbling along in tank mode. "Why are we looking so hard for one lousy runaway Autobot?"

Ruckus rattled slightly. It could have been a pothole in the road, or anxiety that Megatron would explode in a rage at having to explain his plan yet again. Megatron, however, stayed calm. The days of his furious, uncontrolled outbursts were over. Megatron had seen the future, seen what he was to become. His destiny as Galvatron, the all-powerful future Decepticon leader awaited him, and while he would never suffer fools gladly he now had the self-

assurance to deal tactfully with minds like Quake's, which were vastly inferior to his own. "My dear Quake," he began, "anti-robot feeling amongst the humans has never been higher following the damage inflicted upon Rivers' Town. I intend to capitalise on this mania by capturing and publically dealing with the errant Autobot. This will show the humans that Prime's force has been their real enemy all along. Having thus gained the humans' support, I'll have a power base to confront not only Prime's Autobots but also the two renegade factions within the Decepticons, led by Scorponok and Shockwave. Of course, once the humans have outlived their usefulness, they'll join Prime, Scorponok and Shockwave – on the scrap heap!"

"Nice one, Boss," Quake grunted as the Decepticon force rolled on into the night. "It's got real, y'know, vision. I guess that guy Galvatron you're always on about would approve too."

"I do!" Megatron replied, and the Walther P-38 quivered with chilling, menacing laughter once more.

B ackstreet quivered with nervous tension. The pin-pricks of light had become

pencil-torch beams as the headlights of his hunters moved inexorably closer. The Triggerbot strained his optical sensors to discern what the vehicles approaching were. Was that a tank? Yes – unmistakable now, as he heard its dull rumbling thunder motors. Backstreet immediately thought of the Autobot, Warpath – but then he spotted other military vehicles, and he had it at last – the Combaticons! The Decepticons had put a Special Team, a bunch of real heavies, on his tail. Well if they wanted him that bad, he wasn't going to disappoint them by surrendering without a fight.

Backstreet transformed back to sports car mode, taking care to keep his own headlights off. He began creeping back towards his pursuers, straining to remember the twists and turns of the mountain road along which he'd raced for his life minutes earlier.

Backstreet saw the headlights of his hunters disappear as the road took them into the mountain. They'd next appear coming around that tight bend twenty metres ahead. Backstreet paused, keeping his engine quietly humming. If this was going to work, it would all be in the timing. "Hang on! Hang on just one more minute!" Backstreet urged himself for the second time that night. Then suddenly his rear rocket thrusters exploded into life. Backstreet hurtled forward, keeping his lights off.

He powered to the crown of the bend, determined not to lose control this time. The beams from the headlights of the others illuminated the contours of the road for him from the far side. He was still accelerating when the vehicles came into view, just metres from his bumpers. Backstreet's heat-ray headlights instantly flared, burning deep gouges into the first of the convoy. His wing-mounted proton missile cannons were pounding away, missing more than hitting, but creating a devastating protective barrage. Behind this arrow-wedge of explosive power, the Triggerbot roared on at ever increasing speed, knifing through the ranks of military vehicles. Amid the chaos, amid the shrieking, grating cacophony of proton cannoned, heat-ray scorched metal, Backstreet heard cries of pain and anguish. As he finally cleared the hunting pack, rocketting down the mountain road, Backstreet's grim satisfaction at another narrow escape began to diminish when it dawned on him that the howls he'd heard from the carnage he'd created. . . had been from humans!

Megatron greeted the news of the Autobot's unprovoked attack on the human military convoy with demonic relish. "This hapless Triggerbot is doing my work for me," he told the grinning Ruckus a day after the event. "I scarcely need to convince the humans who their real enemy is now – this latest act of Autobot terrorism is undeniable evidence. Backstreet has played right into my hands."

"Backstreet's actions have tied my hands," concluded Prime solemnly as he digested the same information. "I cannot allow a rogue Autobot to continue harassing humans. It was an astounding miracle that no soldier was killed"

"But what can we do to stop him?" asked the anxious Override.

"We can re-double our efforts to track Backstreet down," Prime responded. "And if it's clear that he is totally beyond reason. . . we must terminate him!"

Continued on page 43.

AUTOBOT: RACE CAR PATROL

ROADHANDLER – "Unwary warriors soon become wrecks." *TAILSPIN* – **"Put the pedal to the metal."** *FREEWHEELER* – "Avoid the potholes on the road of life." *SWINDLER* – **"Burn rubber, not energon."**

The Race Car Patrol's primary function is reconnaissance, and their team motto ("In confusion there is opportunity.") sums up their general outlook on life as much as their approach to a battle. Fast and fearless, the quartet will check out battle sites for the big guns, but don't mind mixing it up with any early-arriving Decepticons. Led by the free-spirited, Roadhandler, the group pretty much do their own thing. They can be guided but not controlled. They like to think of themselves as a mini commando unit, affiliated to the main Autobot army. The Race Car Patrol use their superior manoeuvrability and instinctive understanding of any terrain to harass the enemy and lead them into difficult situations. Their hit and run policy has proved very successful. A vital component of the Autobot ranks. All take great pride in their work.

AUTOBOT: OFF ROAD PATROL

POWERTRAIN – "If I can't go through it, I go over it." *MUDSLINGER* – "No foe is too tough". *HIGHJUMP* – "Keep it down and dirty." *TOTE* – "No road is too rough, no foe is too tough. Boldly announcing A rolling Autobot gathers the most Decepticons."

This foursome make the Race Car Patrol look positively obedient. The Off Road Patrol have an independence streak that runs as long as the Appalachian Trail. And what's more, they're proud of it. Boldly announcing "Don't follow orders, follow instincts" As they go into battle, the Off Road Patrol are difficult, but vitally important and skilled warriors. Specialising in covert operations, the group enjoy going where no-one's ever gone and doing what no-one's ever done. Continually caught up in some sort of enemy intrigue, the Off Road Patrol always work well together. Four thoroughly independent and relentless characters who somehow manage to get along just fine. All perhaps are united by the common desire to wreck as many Decepticons as possible. Autobot Command trusts them to come up with brilliant counter-measures to be sprung on the Decepticons.

Script **SIMON FURMAN** ▼ Art **DAN REED** ▼ Letters **GLIB** ▼ Colour **EUAN PETERS**

DISENGAGE, *DARKWING*, DISENGAGE! YOU'RE TAKING ME DOWN WITH YOU!

CAN'T DISENGAGE! THE SYSTEMS THAT BOND OUR JET FORMS INTO DREADWING HAVE *FUSED!*

WE'RE GOING UNDER–

KA-SPASH!

SILVERBOLT, DID YOU–?

I HEARD, *FIREFLIGHT*, I HEARD! SO DID *OPTIMUS PRIME* ... AND HE'S *NOT* HAPPY!

YOU WERE SUPPOSED TO CRIPPLE DREADWING AND FORCE HIM TO RETURN HERE, NOT *BURY* HIM AT THE BOTTOM OF THE OCEAN!

SILVERBOLT'S RIGHT! YOU AND *SKYDIVE* MAY HAVE SENTENCED A HUMAN TO *DEATH!*

HIQ– HOW'S OUR PATIENT?

NOT GOOD, PRIME. WITHOUT THE *POWER CELL*, ALL THIS FANCY *NEBULAN* TECHNOLOGY IS JUST SO MUCH *WINDOW DRESSING*!

IF WE DON'T GET IT BACK, THE HUMAN'S AS GOOD AS *DEAD!*

THEN GET IT BACK WE WILL... OR PERISH IN THE ATTEMPT! JOIN US OUT HERE, HiQ, WE'RE GOING FOR A *SWIM!*

YOU MEAN WE'RE GOING INTO THAT *WET STUFF*? *YOU CANNOT BE SERIOUS!* I'LL *RUST!*

I'M *DEADLY* SERIOUS, *GETAWAY*. THE HUMAN LYING INJURED IN THIS HOSPITAL IS THERE BECAUSE OF *US!*

JOYRIDE'S PURSUIT OF THE *DECEPTICON*, *QUAKE*, RESULTED IN A HUMAN VEHICLE BEING KNOCKED FROM THE ROAD. THE DRIVER WAS LEFT BARELY ALIVE!

ANOTHER *INNOCENT* VICTIM OF THE WAR *WE AUTOBOTS* BROUGHT TO EARTH!

EXCEPT THAT THIS TIME, USING TECHNOLOGY FROM OUR HOME-WORLD, *NEBULOS*, WE COULD HAVE SAVED HIM.

UNTIL, OF COURSE, *THROTTLE* STOLE THE VITAL COMPONENT!

BEFORE WE REALISED WHAT WAS HAPPENING, DARKWING'S *NEBULAN COMPANION* HAD BROKEN IN AND STOLEN THE POWER CELL!

HE AND *HI-TEST* CAN ABSORB NEAT ENERGY FROM THE CELL, THEREBY MEETING THE DEMANDS OF A DECEPTICON POWERMASTER ENGINE *WITHOUT* HAVING TO CONSUME VAST AMOUNTS OF FOOD!

MAKES ME *ASHAMED* TO BE A NEBULAN! LET'S GO GET THAT ISOTOPE!

LEAPING INTO THE AIR, HiQ *TRANSFORMS*—LANDING AS OPTIMUS PRIME'S *POWERMASTER ENGINE!*

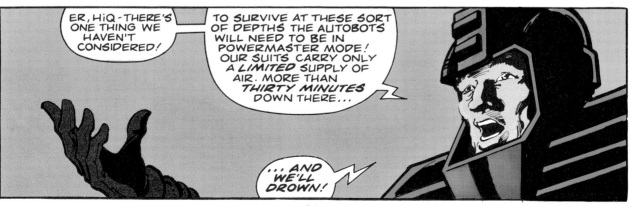

ER, HiQ—THERE'S ONE THING WE HAVEN'T CONSIDERED!

TO SURVIVE AT THESE SORT OF DEPTHS THE AUTOBOTS WILL NEED TO BE IN POWERMASTER MODE! OUR SUITS CARRY ONLY A *LIMITED* SUPPLY OF AIR. MORE THAN *THIRTY MINUTES* DOWN THERE...

...AND WE'LL DROWN!

SOON... THAT'S THE LAST ONE!

REMEMBER, *SLAPDASH*, USE YOUR *INTERNAL SPEAKERS* TO COMM-UNICATE.

GOTCHA, PRIME ...OOPS!

I MEAN, *GOTCHA, PRIME!*

I'M HOMING IN ON YOUR BEACON. HAVE YOU FOUND HIM YET?

YES. THE *AERIALBOTS* GOT A PRETTY GOOD FIX ON DREADWING'S POSITION WHEN HE WENT DOWN. JUST LET YOURSELF DRIFT AND—

PRIME!

WE'VE GOT COMPANY!

WELL, WELL! LOOKS LIKE WE'RE NOT THE ONLY ONES AFTER OUR DEAR COMRADE, DREADWING, EH, SKALOR?

HEE, HEE! RIGHT, SNAP TRAP. LOOKS LIKE A ROUTINE SALVAGE JOB...

...JUST GOT INTERESTING!

REMEMBER, OUR ORDERS ARE TO SECURE THE POWER CELL AND BRING DREADWING TO THE SURFACE! THE FIRST IS ESSENTIAL...

...THE SECOND ISN'T!

SEACONS! WHOA! THANKS, PRIME!

HOW CAN WE BEAT THESE GUYS? THEY'RE BUILT FOR UNDERSEA COMBAT—WE'RE NOT!

BETTER BELIEVE IT, AUTO-WRECK!

I DON'T MEAN TO SHOCK YOU...BUT YOU'RE WAY OUT OF YOUR DEPTH!

REAHHH!

THAT'S IT, *TENTAKIL*, HOLD HIM THERE! *OVERBITE* WANTS TO SINK HIS TEETH INTO—

UH, HI GUYS —I'M HERE—

GNNG!

OOPS! PARDON MY FEET!

NICE TIMING, SLAPDASH!

WHAM!

BUT—

HUH?

THAT'S SKALOR OUT FOR THE COUNT, BUT IT'S A SMALL VICTORY! WE'RE *BADLY OUTCLASSED* DOWN HERE IN THE SEACONS' HOME TERRITORY!

WHAM!

AAH! MY LEG!

HAVING TROUBLE, PRIME? SEAWING'S STING *PARALYSES* ON CONTACT... OR HAD YOU NOTICED?

GOT TO DO SOMETHING ... AND *FAST!* OUR NEBULAN COMPANIONS ARE DOWN TO LESS THAN *HALF A TANK* OF AIR. IF WE FIGHT ON, THEY WILL SURELY DROWN!

WOOMAH!

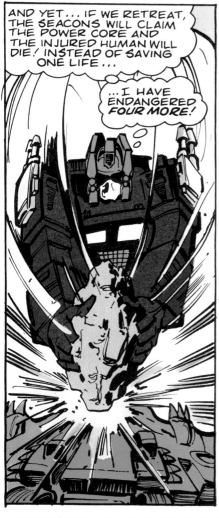

AND YET... IF WE RETREAT, THE SEACONS WILL CLAIM THE POWER CORE AND THE INJURED HUMAN WILL DIE! INSTEAD OF SAVING ONE LIFE...

...I HAVE ENDANGERED *FOUR MORE!*

UNLESS...

HiQ—*TRANSFORM.* YOU AND YOUR FELLOW NEBULANS MUST—

I UNDERSTAND YOUR INTENTIONS PRIME—AND I *REFUSE!*

YOU WISH US TO SECURE THE POWER CORE AND HEAD FOR THE SURFACE, LEAVING YOU TO FACE THE SEACONS *ALONE!*

THERE *HAS* TO BE ANOTHER WAY!

WITHOUT US BOOSTING YOUR POWER AT THESE DEPTHS, YOU'LL BE EASY MEAT FOR THE SEACONS! *HANG* THE DANGER TO US, I SAY WE—

NO! THERE IS MORE AT STAKE HERE THAN JUST *YOUR* LIVES!

37

IF THE HUMAN DIES BECAUSE *I* FAILED TO ACT, THEN EVEN IF WE WIN THIS BATTLE — WE HAVE *LOST!*

PLEASE, HiQ — SUMMON YOUR FELLOW NEBULANS!

AND, MOMENTS LATER...

HURRY, *HOTWIRE!*

KEEP YOUR ARMOUR ON, *REV*, I'M GOING AS FAST AS I...

...*CAN?*

WHOAA!

NO WAY, HiQ, YOU'RE NOT HAVING THE ISOTOPE. I'LL—

THROTTLE...

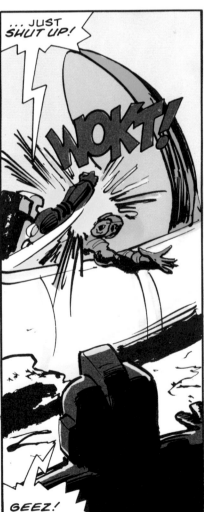

...JUST *SHUT UP!*

WOKT!

GEEZ!

THOUGH NORMALLY VIOLENCE IS AGAINST MY NATURE, HI-TEST, THIS ONCE I'M WILLING TO MAKE AN *EXCEPTION!*

AAHUURK! TAKE IT, *TAKE IT!*

PERHAPS THERE IS YET A WAY TO SAVE THE AUTOBOTS!

I COULD *ABSORB* THE POWER CORE'S ENERGY. COMBINED WITH PRIME HE'D HAVE ACCESS TO *LIMITLESS* ENERGY. ENOUGH TO DEFEAT THE SEACONS!

A MERE *THREE MINUTES* OF AIR LEFT. AH WELL, WHO WANTS TO LIVE FOREVER?

BUT... HOW WILL USING THE POWER CORE FOR MY OWN PURPOSES MAKE ME ANY BETTER THAN THE DECEPTICONS?

PRIME CERTAINLY *WOULD'NT* THANK ME!

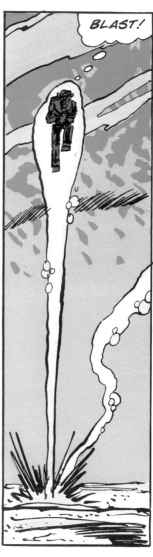

BLAST!

39

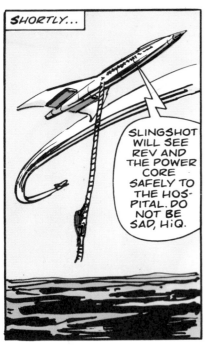

SHORTLY...

SLINGSHOT WILL SEE REV AND THE POWER CORE SAFELY TO THE HOSPITAL. DO NOT BE SAD, HiQ.

THOUGH OUR SEARCH PROVED *NEGATIVE*, WE CAN BE HEARTENED BY KNOWING THAT PRIME DIED AS HE WOULD HAVE WANTED, SAVING THE LIFE OF ANOTHER.

I SUPPOSE SO, SILVERBOLT.

IF NOTHING ELSE, I'VE LEARNT A NEW PERSPECTIVE ON LIFE. NO MATTER HOW PRECIOUS IT IS TO US, IT BECOMES WASTED IF WE FORGET OUR RESPONSIBILITY TO OTHERS!

I COULDN'T HAVE PUT IT BETTER MYSELF, HiQ!

PRIME AND THE OTHERS ...BUT *HOW*-?

YOU NEGLECTED TO SHUT DREADWING'S HATCH. HAVING LOST THE POWER CORE, THE SEACONS DECIDED THEY COULDN'T AFFORD TO LET HI-TEST AND THROTTLE DROWN!

ERM, PRIME - COULD WE DISCUSS THIS LATER? I WAS RIGHT ABOUT THIS WET STUFF...

...I'M STARTING TO *RUST*!

THE END!

WHO WON THE DUEL OF WITS?

Well, you won't know that until you've checked off your answers against those below. If you're wondering what we're on about, it means you're reading this annual out of sequence. If you haven't played the *Autobot Versus Decepticon – Duel of Wits* yet, read no further until you have (it can be found on pages 20 & 21). Right, for those of you who have played the game, or are in the process of playing the game – here's your guide to the answers. Below, left are the names of Autobots A – D. *Only* the Decepticon player should look at these, checking that his opponent is correctly identifying his warriors before asking their questions. Below, right are the names of Decepticons A – D. These are for the Autobot player's sole use. Below these are the answers to each set of questions (Autobot questions, left, and Decepticon questions, right).

AUTOBOT A – **BLASTER**
AUTOBOT B – **JAZZ**
AUTOBOT C – **OMEGA SUPREME**
AUTOBOT D – **GRIMLOCK**

DECEPTICON A – DEVASTATOR
DECEPTICON B – BLITZWING
DECEPTICON C – DIVE BOMB
DECEPTICON D – HEADSTRONG

Autobot A answers: 1) Optimus Prime; 2) Ratchet; 3) The Creation Matrix. **Autobot B answers:** 1) Auntie; 2) Swoop; 3) Fire engine. **Autobot C answers:** 1) Galvatron; 2) Death's Head – Goldbug; 3) Ethan Zachary. **Autobot D answers:** 1) Unicron; 2) Hot Rod – Rodimus Prime; 3) Cyclonus.

Decepticon A answers: 1) An asteroid field; 2) Ravage; Walther P-38. **Decepticon B answers:** 1) Laserbeak and Buzzsaw; 2) Sparkplug Witwicky; 3) Vortex – Bruticus. **Decepticon C answers:** 1) Fracas and nightstick; 2) Dreadwing; 3) By possessing Megatron. **Decepticon D answers:** 1) Soundwave; 2) The Quintessons; 3) Shockwave.

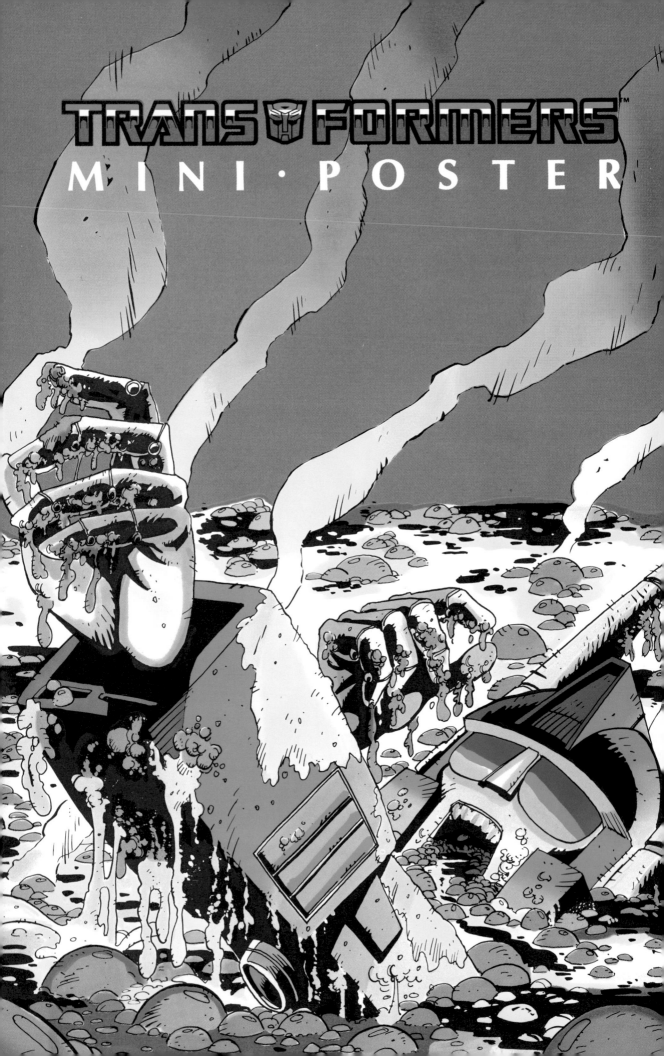

TRIGGER -HAPPY!
PART 2

Story: DAN ABNETT
Art: ART WETHERELL/
STEPHEN BASKERVILLE

Night Watchman, Don Stracher, stifled another yawn and headed west across the twilit fairground. His motor tricycle allowed him to speed around the deserted buildings and arcades during his shift, to check for any intruders who may come to grief fooling on the unsafe frameworks of the rusty rides.

But there was seldom any trouble. Riverway Fun Park had closed six years before, and since then its only visitors had been the odd group of high school kids from nearby Rivers' Town, who once in a blue moon would come up here after the bars had all shut. Those blue moons had become very infrequent these days.

Bored, and wishing just a little for some excitement, Don pulled up by the doors of the Cyclorama 3-D cinema. The shutters were ajar. Curious, Don approached. Sure enough, someone had forced the lock . . . no, scratch that . . . someone had *crushed* the lock in order to gain access.

Don hefted his flashlight and stepped into the darkness. He chewed his gum aggressively before crying out a challenge to whoever was inside. School kids he could handle . . . drunks or tramps too. Even petty thieves offered no serious problem to him.

The massive, ultra-sophisticated humanoid robot that he found with his flashlight

was just a little out of his league.

"Wait! I don't . . .'' cried the equally alarmed Backstreet.

But Don Stracher had already had quite enough excitement for one night and was running, screaming out of the fairground.

A few miles distant, a great pall of dust rose from the highway and blotted out the setting sun. At a pace that emphasised their urgency, the massed Autobot convoy thundered on in search of their rogue team-mate, Backstreet. As they raced along in their vehicle modes, the Autobots' robotic sensors scanned the area around them; sight, sound, heat tell-tales, and listened out to the broadcasts on radio and television right across the spectrum. In the mind of the majority of Autobots present, Triggerbots and Double Targetmasters alike, there had formed a simple determination about their mission: Backstreet had stepped out of line and had fled. It was up to them to find him, straighten him out, and help him find his confidence again. As an Autobot, even a wayward one, he deserved no less.

The team leader, Optimus Prime, raced along at the head of the convoy, in the guise of the mighty road train. His thoughts on the whole, messy affair were decidedly more muddied than most of his colleagues. Backstreet was rogue, endangering human life through his rash actions. He was in danger of falling prey to Decepticon wiles . . . maybe even joining the Decepticons in an effort to escape Autobot justice. But justice had to be done; Backstreet needed to be severely reprimanded. Indeed, thought Prime, if he refuses to surrender to our custody, then his punishment would be very severe. But Prime was determined to help the fleeing Autobot, to try and discover why his failure at the ambush had prompted him to flee so desperately instead of admitting his guilt and accepting a simple reprimand.

One other present had troubled thoughts. Override mulled over his earlier goading of the ashamed Backstreet and his exaggerated claims that Prime was so cross with Backstreet that he would order the Triggerbot's termination. Should he speak up? Confess? Explain the true cause of Backstreet's panic? Or would it be safer, for himself, in the long run . . . to stay silent? Override thought back to Prime's grim face as the search began. Yes, it probably was better to stay as quiet as possible . . .

The dying sunlight found out the sleek form of another robot near the fair-

ground. But this was Spinister, the Decepticon scout, hovering high up in his stealth mode, attack helicopter shape. His hypersensitive scanners were picking up a radio broadcast from a human called Don Stracher who was frantically calling up the local police about a 'monster robot man' he had discovered in the Riverway Fun Park.

"Spinister to Megatron," breathed Spinister into his tranceiver, "This is the news you've been waiting for: I've found our trigger-happy runaway . . .!"

Racked by a deeper loneliness than he had ever known, Backstreet crept from the Cyclorama into the cool evening air. A winking light in the purple west made him start in fear, but he reassured himself. It was just a human helicopter on its way home. He was alone here. Especially now that poor human had run off.

So deeply wrapped in his own misery was Backstreet, that he didn't notice the blinking light in the night sky bank towards the fairground and start to come his way.

"Megatron to all Decepticon units. Target is located. Do not, repeat do not molest him until I arrive. Megatron out." Spinister smiled as he listened to the instructions over the radio. Sure he wouldn't molest the poor lost Autobot, just rough him up a little, maybe force him to join the Decepticons before Megatron even arrived. Such a stark display of initiative would probably get him a hefty promotion.

Spinister banked lower. To the east, he saw a yellow construction excavator trundling off the road towards the fairground.

"Yo, Spinister!" called Scoop, "Am I the first to arrive?"

"Confirmed, Scoop." responded Spinister, "Fancy bagging this runaway with me?"

"You heard what Megatron said . . ." replied the excavator.

"Forget it." snapped Spinister. "Let's show him he can count on his troops to get the job done! GERONIMO!"

Backstreet wheeled as he heard the battle 'copter screaming down at him, deadly lasers stitching a tracered line across the grass of the fairground. He returned fire instinctively and tried to find cover. The Decepticon chopper neatly sidestepped his wild shots and swung in low to flush him out from the dim funhouse blocks. 'If I can just get him crosshaired . . .' muttered Backstreet as Spinister edged nearer and nearer into his sights. But then the Autobot's world dissolved in a welter of flame and shattered steel. He rolled frantically from the massive multiple blasts that had rent asunder one of the funhouse buildings and saw Scoop, in robot form, taking aim with Holepunch, his steel-breaking dual compression cannon. 'Yee-hah!' exclaimed Scoop, "Time to die, Autobot!"

Some miles away, the fast approaching night seemed to counterpoint Optimus Prime's darkening mood. The search for Backstreet had frayed the tempers of all the Autobots, but Prime had – until moments ago – held his in leaderly restraint. But now, standing with the others in a windswept cornfield, Prime's temper was about to break in the face of Override's little confession.

"You did what?!" Exclaimed Prime incredulously.

"I guess I should have mentioned it before now ..." began Override, but Prime wasn't listening. He gazed into the distance, bracing himself mentally for the dire consequences of Override's actions . . .

Backstreet braced himself for the blasts he knew must soon come, but suddenly a new figure, vast and menacing loomed behind Scoop. The hovering Spinister was knocked sideways through the sky by an almost dismissive blow, and Scoop was hauled bodily off the ground – a vice-like hand gouging deep indents into the metal of his neck.

"SCOOP! SPINISTER! You fools!" roared the newcomer, "Back off now, completely, and don't show your faces for a very long time! Don't ever disobey my orders again!"

Backstreet cowered. This was it. The end. There was no mistaking the huge figure before him . . .

"Megatron . . ." he whispered.

"Tell me exactly what you said to Backstreet", demanded Optimus Prime, at last mastering his emotions and thoughts. He fixed Override with a baleful stare, waiting.

"I said . . . er . . . that you were a little cross with him for disobeying orders . . . and that he would probably get court martialed . . ."

"How could you, Override?" snapped Scoop, "You know what a short fuse that Triggerbot's got!"

"I-I didn't really think." said Override." Look, Prime, I'm afraid I also said that you'd probably order his termination . . ."

There was a long silence broken only by the whisper of wind in the corn and a long, low whistle of amazement from Landfill.

"No wonder he ran." said Prime at last." In the face of that verdict he may jump at *any* chance to escape . . . even joining the Decepticons!

Megaron stepped forward. Backstreet cowered down. Megatron stretched out his hand, and an uncharacteristic smile crossed his face. Megatron spoke, "Join us, my friend!"

"**P**rime!" called Dogfight, and the Autobot team looked up to where the airborne Autobot hovered above the cornfield. "I've just intercepted a transmission from Spinister, the Decepticon scout, to Megatron. He's found Backstreet in a fairground near here, and Megatron's on his way there now."

"Feed me the co-ordinates." replied Prime. "I'm on my way. The rest of you, stay here! If we show up in numbers, Backstreet will fear the worst! It's up to me to straighten this thing out . . . alone!"

"**O**uch," whispered Quake to his fellow Decepticon, Needlenose, as they looked on from a distance. "If ol' Mega-mouth tries to look any more sincere, his face'll rust!"

"I just feel sorry for that poor Autobot fool!" replied Needlenose." He thinks it's all for real. He doesn't know what's in store for him if he gives in!"

Megatron turned his head a little to one side, and smiled sensitively. "Look, Backstreet. I've ordered all my troops to remain outside the edge of the fairground whilst we talk, as a gesture of goodwill. I can make you a genuine offer of protection, and a place in a crack Decepticon team if you join me. Now what do you say? Is that not a fine offer?"

Backstreet had backed away from the vast Decepticon leader into the shadow of the heltersketer and he glanced nervously at Megatron. "Oh-oh . . . it sure sounds like a swell offfer, Decepticon, and you're right, I am in a pretty bad spot. But join the Decepticons? I d-don't know about that . . ."

"What is there to know? The choice seems obvious." Megatron's smile gleamed, "You join us . . . or you're dead!"

"If that's a theat, then you've made a mistake, Megatron," said Backstreet, finding a last reserve of courage from somewhere.

"If I'm going to die, I'd rather it be as an official punishment termination for my crimes than a slow death at the hands of you Decepticons."

"Ideals!" grinned Megatron, "So many ideals. Think carefully, Backstreet – what's best for you? Think . . . take your time."

Time was running out, and Prime knew it. As his Nebulan companion, HiQ – nestling under Prime's bodywork in engine mode – struggled to meet his Powermaster's demands for energy, Prime poured on the speed. A nasty seed of dread had borne fruit in his mind. He knew the mind of Megatron – his oldest and deadliest enemy – almost as well as he knew his own, and doubted Megatron would pass up such a superb opportunity to subvert an Autobot warrior. If he succeeded in turning a single Autobot to the Decepticon cause, the ultimate victory would be his! As Prime neared the fairground, his worst fears were given shape and form. There was Megatron, extending a friendly hand to Backstreet. Prime smashed through the makeshift barrier formed by Ruckus and Quake and entered the fairground. The sight which met his eyes boosted his flagging spirits . . .

Backstreet shrugged and turned away from Megatron, telling Megatron to do his worst.

"I may not be the world's best Autobot, Megatron," he said with a rueful smile, "but I'm no Decepticon, that's for sure!"

Megatron just snarled, raising a vast fist to strike Backstreet down.

A commanding voice froze the blow in mid-air!

"Prime!" spat Megatron, spinning to face his oldest, deadliest rival. "You've made a grave mistake in coming here alone, Autobot!"

"I'm here to help a fellow warrior." said Prime sternly. "Now stand aside, Megatron."

"You'll have to go through me." replied the Decepticon darkly. The ground around Prime erupted under heavy fire as Megatron's Decepticon team launched an offensive to protect their leader.

"Back! Get back!" screamed Megatron, heaving his own weaponry to bear. "Prime is mine!"

The Decepticon warriors skidded to a halt and watched in wonder as Megatron leapt for Prime's throat. Prime's concussion blaster ripped fragments from Megatron's armour, but still the two mighty warriors crashed together and went down in a blurr of flailing limbs that completely obliterated a shooting gallery.

There can be few sights more awesome

than the clash of two of the most powerful robot beings in the Universe. The ground shook as though gripped by an earthquake as the two of them wrestled for a better hold, too close were the quarters for their laser weapons.

"You're weakening, Prime!" growled Megatron.

"You're fantasising, Megatron!" snapped Prime, but he could not avoid the fist that smashed him backwards through the scaffolded side of the roller coaster. Megatron plunged after him to press his advantage.

Nearby, Backstreet ran desperately for cover as the terrible clash continued to explode behind him. "Oh what have I done?" he asked himself, "What have I done?!?"

With a snarl, Optimus Prime swung the shredded frame of the Ferris Wheel against his foe and smashed him to the ground. In an instant, Megatron was on his feet again, ripping through the twisted metal, wrenching off one of the Ferris wheel cars and hurling it like a beachball at Prime. Caught unawares, the car hammered into the side of his face. Prime staggered under the impact and fell against the dodgems shed. Megatron seemed unstoppable.

A supreme confidence flooded through Megatron's circuits as he lunged forward. He knew he could not lose, for his glorious future as the mighty Galvatron was already preordained. Prime, though, poor Optimus Prime . . . he had already tasted death once on Earth! How easy it would be for him to die again!

"Fool!" bellowed Megatron, crushing a dodgem car into a ball and throwing it at Prime. "You with your foolish sense of duty! You battle for an Autobot that you were prepared to terminate!"

Prime redoubled his efforts despite his swimming head. His blows drove Megatron back a pace. "We would only have initiated termination if all attempts to reason with him had failed! Backstreet could have been spoken to, made to see sense!"

"Pah!" spat Megatron, landing a punch that sent the Autobot reeling. "Backstreet is an Autobot no longer. He would never have responded to your talk. He was all set to join us when you arrived!"

Prime sank to his knees and struggled to rise again. Megatron was closing. "You're wrong." he gasped. "I believe Backstreet is still a virtuous individual. If he had gone bad, he wouldn't have wasted a moment in joining you. If he had to think, then there's still hope. If there's still hope, he's still

worth fighting for!"

So saying, Prime launched himself desperately at his foe. But Megatron met his onslaught calmly. His first blow stopped Prime in his tracks, his second rocked him backwards. Then Megatron reached out a fist and grabbed Prime by the throat, pinning the dazed Autobot still. There was hum as Megatron charged up his fusion cannon and placed the muzzle calmly at Prime's head.

"It's over, Prime." he said.

The double proton blast caught Megatron unawares and knocked him bodily across the torn up funfair. Shocked and bewildered, Prime tried to find his feet, looking over at where a singed and astonished Megatron was himself trying to rise.

"Come on, Sir! Come on!" implored a voice from behind Prime. Prime turned. "Backstreet! What in the name of Matrix . . .?"

"I heard what you said . . . I saw the way you kept fighting. I couldn't just watch any longer!"

"Thank goodness you acted when you did. I could have been spare parts in another moment!" Prime managed a smile despite the dents in his face plating and the oil running down his temple.

"Still could happen!" cried Backstreet,

pointing. "Megatron may be out for the count, but his friends sure as heck aren't!"

True enough, the two Autobots could see the cavalcade of Decepticons coming their way. Prime just smiled. "If I can't handle this lot then I'd better give up Transformer warfare for good!"

Prime transformed to battle station mode, unleashing his massive arsenal of lasers, particle beam cannons and concussion blasters. The Decepticons were sent howling and running for cover.

"Now!" ordered Prime. "Transform to car mode, Backstreet, while we have a chance! Let's go!"

In an instant the two vehicles were speeding out of the ruined funfair. Backstreet in his sports car mode, and Prime and his nebulan companion, HiQ, transformed and combined into their powerful articulated road train.

"Stop them!" bellowed Megatron from his prone position, "Stop them now!"

But the Autobots had already escaped.

A hush fell across the sparse debate chamber at the Autobots' base. All optics were on the lone figure who stood in the centre of the circular room in a pool of warm amber light. Backstreet was silent for a long while, and then he raised his head and spoke solemnly.

"Fellow Autobots. I understand the charges that have been levelled against me; namely disobeying a direct order from Optimus Prime and also attacking the human army convoy and therefore endangering human life in a wholesale and careless manner.

I offer no defence of my actions which I now very much regret. I plead guilty to both charges as read."

A murmur ran through the chamber that immediately silenced as Optimus Prime rose to speak. Prime's face was grave, the atmosphere dreadfully tense.

"Fellow Autobots . . . friends. In the face of the plea of guilty, I must pass sentence."

The Autobots craned forward and hung upon Prime's every word.

"These are extremely serious crimes, for which there can be only one sentence: this just be the termination . . ."

There was a gasp from the Autobots.

". . . of Backstreet's role as a solo look-out!" Prime smiled at the assembled crowd. "In future, when radio silence is being maintained, the vital responsibility for look-out duty will be shared. No one Autobot will ever be isolated in such a position again."

There was cheering and applauding from the crowd. Backstreet shook his head in disbelief. "Thankyou, Sir . . ." he began.

"Not at all." replied Prime, "Thank*you*, Autobot!"

THE END!

DECEPTICON: AIR STRIKE PATROL

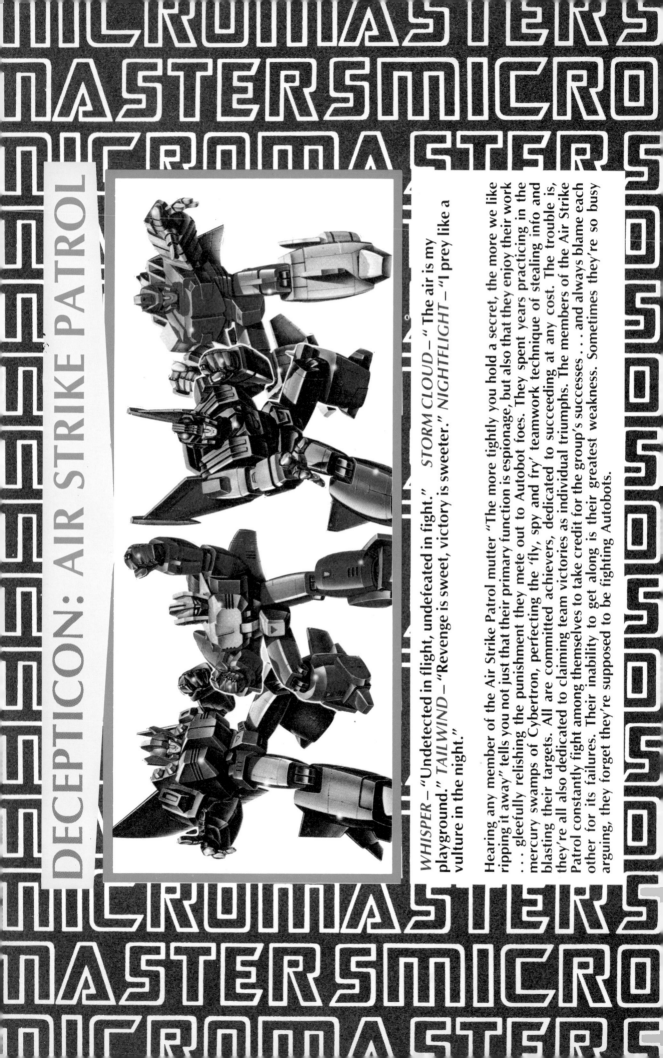

WHISPER – "Undetected in flight, undefeated in fight." *STORM CLOUD* – "The air is my playground." *TAILWIND* – "Revenge is sweet, victory is sweeter." *NIGHTFLIGHT* – "I prey like a vulture in the night."

Hearing any member of the Air Strike Patrol mutter "The more tightly you hold a secret, the more we like ripping it away" tells you not just that their primary function is espionage, but also that they enjoy their work ... gleefully relishing the punishment they mete out to Autobot foes. They spent years practicing in the mercury swamps of Cybertron, perfecting the 'fly, spy and fry' teamwork technique of stealing info and blasting their targets. All are committed achievers, dedicated to succeeding at any cost. The trouble is, they're all also dedicated to claiming team victories as individual triumphs. The members of the Air Strike Patrol constantly fight among themselves to take credit for the group's successes ... and always blame each other for its failures. Their inability to get along is their greatest weakness. Sometimes they're so busy arguing, they forget they're supposed to be fighting Autobots.

DECEPTICON: SPORTS CAR PATROL

BLACKJACK – "The road to victory is paved with Autobot wrecks!" *DETOUR* – "To flee before overwhelming odds is no vice, to stay and be smashed is not virtue." *HYPERDRIVE* – "Whenever I drive, the highway becomes a demolition derby!" *ROAD HUGGER* – "Only cowards stop at red lights!"

Mean, mini-berserkers, all four members of the Sports Car Patrol would rather hit first and ask questions later. In some it's more immediately evident (Hyperdrive has little time for intricate plotting or strategy, understanding only the effectiveness of brute force), in others it's held in check (Blackjack holds the team together and marshals his unit). But it's there all the same . . . the need to smash rather than follow plans is just under the skin in all of them. The group are easily the nastiest machines ever to hit the road. Their prime objective is to clear a route for Decepticon ground forces, and they don't care how many wrecks they leave by the wayside. Known for their menacing clean up tactics, it is speed that is their true calling card. It enables them to swiftly clear anything from their path – eliminating it mercilessly. When they say "It takes force to push back the enemy but speed clears the way" they mean it!

TRANS FORMERS

THE GULF OF NEW MEXICO...

SPOTTER TO BASE. NOW CIRCLING THE *KEELER OIL TERMINAL*. ALL LOOKS QUIET SO FAR—

MY GOD! ER. BASE...

...I THINK WE'VE GOT A *BIG* PROBLEM!

THE CHAIN GANG!

MOVE, *FLESHLINGS!* MY INTERIOR FORM YEARNS FOR THE *BLACK FUEL!* IN THE NAME OF THE *DECEPTICON PRETENDERS*, HURRY!

UNH!

UHK!

URR!

Script **DAN ABNETT** ◆ Art **DAN REED** ◆ Letters **GLIB** ◆ Colour **EUAN PETERS**

SKULLGRIN'S RIGHT, *BOMB-BURST*, THE HUMANS REALLY ARE PAINFULLY *INNEFFI-CIENT!*

PERHAPS, *IGUANUS.* BUT ONCE THIS FINAL COMPONENT IS IN PLACE, THE *TRANS-MUTER* WILL RENDER THEIR CRUDE FUEL ACCEPTABLE TO OUR DELICATE PALATES.

THRAUNGG!

IMBECILES! WORTH-LESS HUMAN *GERMS!* SEEMS IF YOU WANT SOMETHING DONE RIGHT ON THIS PLANET...

RUN! THE BIG ONE'S GONE *CRAZY!*

...YOU HAVE TO DO IT YOURSELF! RAAGH!

KANK!

DID YOU SEE THAT? IT HEFTED THAT THING AS IF IT WEIGHED *NOTHING!*

I REPEAT—GIANT ALIEN CREATURES OF IMMENSE STRENGTH! WE'LL NEED—

HANG ON...

55

KIND OF YOU BOYS TO FINALLY MAKE YOUR MOVE, WE WERE GETTIN' SORT OF *TIRED* FOLLOWING YOU DOWN THE COAST!

I GUESS WHEN YOU'RE LOW ON FUEL, YOU START TO GET *CARELESS!*

RAGH! CARELESS? SHOW YOU CARELESS!

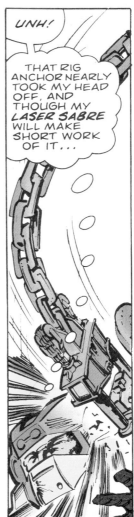

UNH!

THAT RIG ANCHOR NEARLY TOOK MY HEAD OFF, AND THOUGH MY *LASER SABRE* WILL MAKE SHORT WORK OF IT...

FASSH!

...SKULLGRIN'S GOT OTHER TRICKS UP HIS SLEEVE—LIKE SHEDDING HIS OUTER SKIN AND TRANSFORMING TO TANK MODE!

BLAMM!

IF HIS *SHRAPNEL CANNON* SCORES A HIT, I'M FINISHED! GOTTA' MAKE THIS SHOT COUNT!

57

GHAA!

KAMM!

CHZZ

WE'RE HIT!

FOOLISH AUTOBOT. BY GETTING SO CLOSE YOU'VE GIVEN ME A CHANCE TO USE MY RUST INDUCING POWERS!

I'D SHUT UP IF I WERE YOU, AND TAKE A LOOK UPSTAIRS!

THAT PLANE'S GONNA' HIT THE TERMINAL! WE HAVE TO STOP IT AND SAVE THE HUMANS.

ARE YOU MAD? WHY SHOULD I CARE ABOUT THE HUMANS?

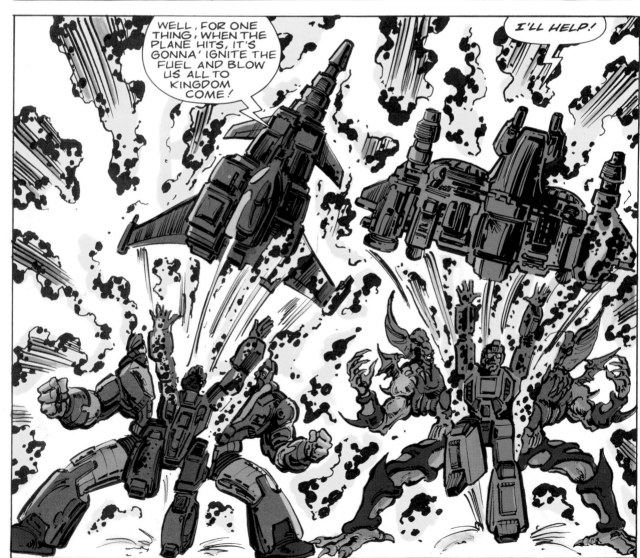

WELL, FOR ONE THING, WHEN THE PLANE HITS, IT'S GONNA' IGNITE THE FUEL AND BLOW US ALL TO KINGDOM COME!

I'LL HELP!

MOMENTS LATER...

THAT'S IT, WE'VE GOT HER! SET HER DOWN GENTLY NOW!

HO!! I MAY BE HELPING YOU, BUT THAT DOESN'T MEAN YOU CAN ORDER ME ABOUT!

WANNA' BET!

I NOTICED THAT MY COLLEAGUES HAD SUBDUED SKULLGRIN AND IGUANUS. THAT JUST LEAVES YOU!

WHAT?

SOON...

HURRY IT UP, DECEPTICONS! AFTER THAT TRANSMUTER IS DISMANTLED YOU'RE OFF TO CYBER-TRON TO FACE TRIAL!

CHARMING! AND AFTER ALL THE HELP I GAVE YOU! YOU AUTOBOTS HAVE NO GRATITUDE!

BOMB-BURST, IF IT'LL MAKE YOU FEEL BETTER... THANKS VERY MUCH!

THE END!

59

AUTOBOT: RESCUE PATROL

SEAWATCH – "Without freedom of the seas, there is no freedom." *STAKEOUT* – "Sometimes you must go outside the law to enforce it." *FIXIT* – "The worst wrecks are my best patients." *RED HOT* – "The hotter things get, the better I like it."

The four members of the Rescue Patrol are indispensable to the Autobot army. On land, or at sea, they are there to administer aid to the injured or assistance to the beleaguered. Though their primary functions are search and rescue, they are all competent warriors in their own right. If they can't save an Autobot comrade, by heck they'll avenge him. All are fully equipped to administer emergency aid under the most adverse conditions (from raging storms to raging battles), and will willingly brave the heaviest combat fire to perform their assigned tasks. To help them back up their assertion that "True victory can only lie in the ability to locate and mend the injured." Seawatch possesses over-the-horizon radar and towing capability, Stakeout has a state-of-the-art communications dashboard, Fixit is outfitted with repair bay and life function monitors, and Red Hot contains fire retardant chemical foam.

AUTOBOT: BATTLE PATROL

BIG SHOT – "One good shot is worth a hundred bad ones!" *SIDETRACK* – A battle that isn't worth winnin' isn't worth fightin'." *SUNRUNNER* – "Rule the skies and the ground will bow before you."

In distinct contrast to the Rescue Patrol, the four members of the Battle Patrol go in with all guns blazing. The Autobots' Rapid Deployment Strike Force (they all agree that "It is better to strike first than not at all") are tough talking, battle-hardened bruisers. To them, the best offensive is one that's fast, furious and ferocious. Don't tell them the odds, just tell them where the enemy is. They won't stop until either the enemy is defeated and thrown on the scrap heap or they are. Defeat is not something they consider, but neither are they afraid to go down in battle. If you've got to go, you've got to go in battle is a sentiment they all share. State-of-the-art firepower and weaponry, combined with thick armour plating makes them an unstoppable force. They've yet to meet an object that can't be moved!